CAMPING JOURNAL & LOGBOOK

CAMPING JOURNAL & LOGBOOK

TRACK ADVENTURES AND RECORD MEMORIES

PAULINE REYNOLDS-NUTTALL

ROCKRIDGE
PRESS

To my husband, Alma, and our children,
who love camping adventures.

- -

For general information on our other products and services or to obtain technical support, please contact our Customer Care Department within the United States at (866) 744-2665, or outside the United States at (510) 253-0500.

Rockridge Press publishes its books in a variety of electronic and print formats. Some content that appears in print may not be available in electronic books, and vice versa.

TRADEMARKS: Rockridge Press and the Rockridge Press logo are trademarks or registered trademarks of Callisto Media Inc. and/or its affiliates, in the United States and other countries, and may not be used without written permission. All other trademarks are the property of their respective owners. Rockridge Press is not associated with any product or vendor mentioned in this book.

Interior and Cover Designer: Alan Carr
Art Producer: Tom Hood
Editor: Georgia Freedman
Production Editor: Holland Baker
Production Manager: Riley Hoffman

Cover illustration © RocketArt/Creative Market.
Interior illustrations used under license from Shutterstock.com and Noun Project. Author photograph courtesy of Marlin Reynolds.

Paperback ISBN: 978-1-63878-036-6
R0

This Journal Belongs To:

....

Contents

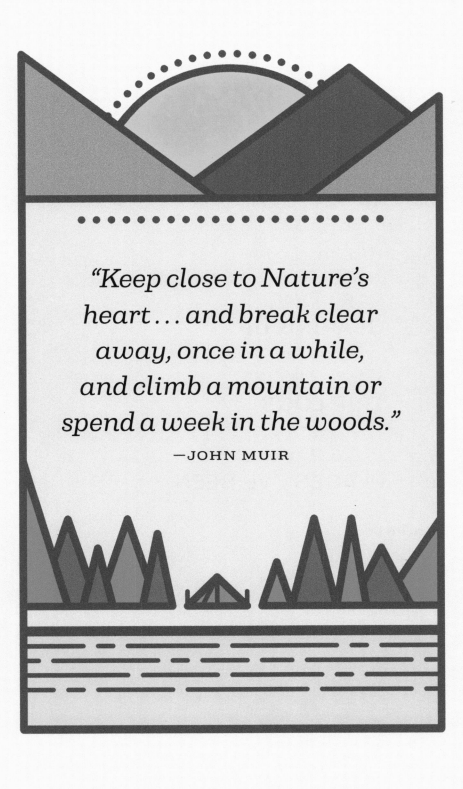

"Keep close to Nature's heart ... and break clear away, once in a while, and climb a mountain or spend a week in the woods."

—JOHN MUIR

How to Use This Book

Welcome to the wonderful world of camping. Getting outside and enjoying the great outdoors with friends and family is one of America's favorite pastimes. Camping in particular is a great way to enjoy Mother Nature's wild landscapes and create great memories.

Our family camps over 40 nights each year. It's a tradition that both my husband and I grew up with. Camping together as a family is something we are both passionate about and that we are passing down to our kids. Our children love camping as much as we do, and I love that we have been able to create some wonderful times for them by introducing them to outdoor adventures. I am also grateful that, through camping, we can help them build skills, teach them values, and show them the benefits of healthy living and the importance of family time.

When my husband and I first started camping with our oldest, we only had my husband's old backpacking gear, which was designed for a single person. It was not practical for a family—nor was the white trash bag we ended up using to carry everything else we needed. Over the years we have learned a few things, including what gear is best for cooking and sleeping outside.

Being prepared is, arguably, the most important part of camping. The second most important (at least for me) is capturing the memories we make on our adventures. One of the best ways to do this is to keep a camping journal or logbook. I keep a little notebook with our camping gear, and I use it to write down the things I forgot to pack, to keep track of our plans, and to jot down important and fun things that happen each day. It was the first thing I bought after that first camping trip we took as a family. I never forget my notebook now because it has become such an important part of my camping kit.

I am hoping that you will find this book as helpful for your adventures as my notebook has been for mine. It's designed not only to help you remember what gear you need but also to let you keep track of where you've been and what you've done. This logbook has helpful checklists, as well as multiple pages with space for documenting weather, campsite reminders, notes, your preferred sites, and more. These pages also have space for writing about the memorable things that happen while camping: who went on the trip, the things you experienced, the animals you saw, and the fun memories you want to hang onto.

It doesn't matter what type of camping you do, whether it's in an RV or a tent. The experience is about communing with nature, connecting with family, and seeing things in a whole different way than you do at home. Camping is an adventure that everyone should experience at least once—and hopefully that first trip will lead to many more! I hope you enjoy and use this camping journal on your next adventure.

LEAVE NO TRACE

When you spend any time outdoors, especially when you're camping, it's important to remember the Leave No Trace principles. These are ethical guidelines that help everyone who enjoys being outside preserve our natural spaces and take care of the great outdoors.

1. **PLAN AHEAD AND PREPARE** – Check the weather and the terrain before you go so that you know what you will need to reduce your impact on the area.

2. **TRAVEL AND CAMP ON DURABLE SURFACES** – Use trails and camping sites that have already been established. Avoid using muddy areas.

3. **DISPOSE OF WASTE PROPERLY** – Leave the area cleaner than when you found it. Remove or dispose of trash and human waste properly. Use available outhouses or pit toilets or dig a cathole as needed.

4. **LEAVE WHAT YOU FIND** – Look at, but don't pick up, the flowers and rocks around you. Leave them so that others can also enjoy them. (If you take these things home, you disrupt natural ecosystems and could also cause the spread of invasive species or bacteria.)

5. **MINIMIZE CAMPFIRE IMPACTS** – Always check fire restrictions in the area prior to starting a fire. Make sure your fire is built in an approved firepit and the area is clear of debris. Never leave a fire unattended, and make sure it is completely out when you leave.

6. **RESPECT WILDLIFE** – Do not feed or harass the animals. Store food properly (in animal-resistant containers such as hung bear bags or bear canisters) any time you are out in the woods so that the wildlife cannot get into it. Food should never be left out.

7. **BE CONSIDERATE OF OTHER VISITORS** – Share the trail. Avoid being a nuisance to other visitors.

Part One

GEARING UP

Before any camping trip, it's important to make sure that you have everything that you need packed and ready. Every type of camping trip is different, so cut from or add to these lists as needed. (To get the most use from these pages, you may want to use a pencil or make photocopies.)

CAMPSITE CHECKLIST

- ☐ Printed site reservation
- ☐ Cash for camping fees
- ☐ Permits, if applicable
- ☐ Tent(s)
- ☐ Tarp(s)
- ☐ Rain fly
- ☐ Tent stakes
- ☐ Sleeping bag(s)
- ☐ Sleeping bag liner(s)
- ☐ Sleeping pad(s)
- ☐ Pillow(s)
- ☐ Guy line or paracord
- ☐ Lantern
- ☐ Flashlights (with extra batteries)
- ☐ Headlamp(s)
- ☐ Water bottle(s)

- ☐ Camping chair(s)
- ☐ Folding table
- ☐ Bucket
- ☐ Shovel
- ☐ Portable power bank
- ☐ Solar charger (and related cords)
- ☐ Hammock
- ☐ Hammock straps
- ☐ Inflatable mattress(es)
- ☐ Camping quilt(s)
- ☐ Camping rug(s)
- ☐ Cot(s)
- ☐ Batteries
- ☐ Leather gloves
- ☐ Portable awning

TOOLS

- ☐ Duct tape
- ☐ Basic tool kit (screwdriver, hammer, nails, etc.)
- ☐ Hatchet or ax
- ☐ Saw

- ☐ Pocketknife
- ☐ Portable jump starter for vehicle (with air hose)
- ☐ Gear repair kit

COOKING EQUIPMENT

- ☐ Water bladder
- ☐ Water purification system
- ☐ Cooler with ice
- ☐ Camp stove
- ☐ Fuel canisters
- ☐ Fire starting kit (tinder, matches, kindling)
- ☐ Bellows
- ☐ Portable grill with pellets or briquettes
- ☐ Grill grate
- ☐ Cooking pan(s), such as cast-iron skillet, frying pan
- ☐ Cooking pot(s), such as Dutch oven, soup/ stockpot
- ☐ Roasting sticks (for hot dogs, s'mores, etc.)
- ☐ Skewers (bamboo or metal, for kebabs)
- ☐ Cooking knife
- ☐ Cutting board
- ☐ Spatula(s) (metal or silicone)
- ☐ Wooden spoon
- ☐ Tongs
- ☐ Can opener

- ☐ Measuring cup(s)
- ☐ Measuring spoons
- ☐ Colander
- ☐ Aluminum foil
- ☐ Coffee maker (such as percolator, French press, pour-over kit)
- ☐ Serving bowl(s)
- ☐ Serving spoon(s)
- ☐ Bowls and plates
- ☐ Utensils
- ☐ Drinking cups
- ☐ Coffee mugs
- ☐ Water jug
- ☐ Collapsible wash basin
- ☐ Dish soap
- ☐ Sponge or dish scrubber
- ☐ Steel wool for cast-iron cookware
- ☐ Dish cloth
- ☐ Reusable (airtight) food storage containers
- ☐ Zip-top bags
- ☐ Garbage bags
- ☐ Collapsible trash can

CLOTHING AND SHOES

- ☐ Hiking boots
- ☐ Thermals
- ☐ Moisture-wicking tops
- ☐ Moisture-wicking shorts
- ☐ Wool socks
- ☐ Underwear
- ☐ Weather- and terrain-appropriate clothing
- ☐ Pajamas
- ☐ Hoodie(s)/Sweater(s)
- ☐ Jacket(s)
- ☐ Raincoat(s)
- ☐ Hat(s)
- ☐ Day pack(s)
- ☐ Sunglasses
- ☐ Bandanna(s)
- ☐ Water shoes
- ☐ Bathing suit(s)
- ☐ Laundry bag
- ☐ Environmentally friendly laundry bar
- ☐ Clothesline

PERSONAL HYGIENE

- ☐ Environmentally friendly soap
- ☐ Toothbrush(es)
- ☐ Toothpaste
- ☐ Environmentally friendly deodorant, shampoo, and conditioner
- ☐ Hand sanitizer
- ☐ Wet wipes
- ☐ Fast-drying towel(s)
- ☐ Hand towel(s)
- ☐ Toilet paper
- ☐ Sunscreen
- ☐ Chapstick
- ☐ Lotion
- ☐ Bug spray
- ☐ Medications
- ☐ Portable toilet
- ☐ Portable shower

SAFETY

- ☐ Bear canister or bear bag
- ☐ Bear spray
- ☐ Safety whistle
- ☐ First aid kit
- ☐ Walkie-talkie

FUN AND ACTIVITIES

- ☐ Field guides
- ☐ Trail maps
- ☐ Binoculars
- ☐ Playing cards
- ☐ Books
- ☐ Portable reader(s) with charger(s) and cords
- ☐ Pen(s) and paper
- ☐ Journal(s)
- ☐ Art supplies
- ☐ Camera (with extra batteries and memory cards)
- ☐ Fishing rod(s)
- ☐ Tackle box
- ☐ Fishing vest(s)
- ☐ Fishing net
- ☐ Fishing license
- ☐ Dry bag
- ☐ Astronomy guide
- ☐ Board games
- ☐ Yard games
- ☐ Portable speaker
- ☐ Glow sticks
- ☐ Bubbles
- ☐ Sand toys
- ☐ Kayak(s)
- ☐ Life jacket(s)
- ☐ Paddleboard(s)
- ☐ Pool floaties/tubes and flotation devices
- ☐ Water guns
- ☐ Bicycle(s)
- ☐ Bicycle pump
- ☐ Bicycle tire repair kit (for bikes and floaties)
- ☐ Pet supplies
- ☐ S'mores kit

Part Two

TRIP LOGS

This section is all about *your* trips and camp-sites. Use the forms below to document your adventures, remind yourself of what you did and didn't like, add tips and important notes for next time, and keep track of all the fun times you've had.

CAMPGROUND/SITE

☆ ☆ ☆ ☆ ☆

Site Name: ....

Contact Info: ....
....

Fees: ....

Dates: ....

Amenities: ....
....
....

Nearby: ....
....

Traveled With/Met: ....
....
....

Weather:

Conditions: ....

Trip Highlights: ....

....

....

Special Conditions/Needs: ....

....

Likes: ....

....

....

Dislikes: ....

....

Notes for Next Time: ....

....

....

THOUGHTS / NOTES / MEMORIES

SKETCHES / MAPS

CAMPGROUND/SITE

☆ ☆ ☆ ☆ ☆

Site Name: ....

Contact Info: ....
....

Fees: ....

Dates: ....

Amenities: ....
....
....

Nearby: ....
....
....

Traveled With/Met: ....
....
....

Weather:

Conditions: ....

Trip Highlights: ....
....
....

Special Conditions/Needs: ....
....

Likes: ....
....
....

Dislikes: ....
....

Notes for Next Time: ....
....
....

THOUGHTS / NOTES / MEMORIES

SKETCHES / MAPS

CAMPGROUND/SITE

☆ ☆ ☆ ☆ ☆

Site Name: ....

Contact Info: ....
....

Fees: ....

Dates: ....

Amenities: ....
....
....

Nearby: ....
....

Traveled With/Met: ....
....
....

Weather:

Conditions: ....

Trip Highlights: ....
....
....

Special Conditions/Needs: ....
....

Likes: ....
....
....

Dislikes: ....
....

Notes for Next Time: ....
....
....

THOUGHTS / NOTES / MEMORIES

SKETCHES / MAPS

CAMPGROUND/SITE

☆ ☆ ☆ ☆ ☆

Site Name: ....

Contact Info: ....
....

Fees: ....

Dates: ....

Amenities: ....
....
....

Nearby: ....
....
....

Traveled With/Met: ....
....
....

Weather:

Conditions: ....

Trip Highlights: ....
....
....

Special Conditions/Needs: ....
....

Likes: ....
....
....

Dislikes: ....
....

Notes for Next Time: ....
....
....

THOUGHTS / NOTES / MEMORIES

SKETCHES / MAPS

CAMPGROUND/SITE

☆ ☆ ☆ ☆ ☆

Site Name: ....

Contact Info: ....
....

Fees: ....

Dates: ....

Amenities: ....
....
....

Nearby: ....
....

Traveled With/Met: ....
....
....

Weather:

Conditions: ....

Trip Highlights: ....
....
....

Special Conditions/Needs: ....
....

Likes: ....
....
....

Dislikes: ....
....

Notes for Next Time: ....
....
....

THOUGHTS / NOTES / MEMORIES

CAMPGROUND/SITE

☆ ☆ ☆ ☆ ☆

Site Name: ....

Contact Info: ....

....

Fees: ....

Dates: ....

Amenities: ....

....

....

Nearby: ....

....

....

Traveled With/Met: ....

....

....

Weather:

Conditions: ....

Trip Highlights: ....

....

....

Special Conditions/Needs: ....

....

Likes: ....

....

....

Dislikes: ....

....

....

Notes for Next Time: ....

....

....

THOUGHTS / NOTES / MEMORIES

SKETCHES / MAPS

CAMPGROUND/SITE

☆ ☆ ☆ ☆ ☆

Site Name: ....

Contact Info: ....

....

Fees: ....

Dates: ....

Amenities: ....

....

....

Nearby: ....

....

Traveled With/Met: ....

....

....

Weather:

Conditions: ....

Trip Highlights: ....

....

....

Special Conditions/Needs: ....

....

Likes: ....

....

....

Dislikes: ....

....

Notes for Next Time: ....

....

....

THOUGHTS / NOTES / MEMORIES

SKETCHES / MAPS

CAMPGROUND/SITE

☆ ☆ ☆ ☆ ☆

Site Name: ....

Contact Info: ....
....

Fees: ....

Dates: ....

Amenities: ....
....
....

Nearby: ....
....

Traveled With/Met: ....
....
....

Weather:

Conditions: ....

Trip Highlights: ....
....
....

Special Conditions/Needs: ....
....

Likes: ....
....
....

Dislikes: ....
....

Notes for Next Time: ....
....
....

THOUGHTS / NOTES / MEMORIES

SKETCHES / MAPS

CAMPGROUND/SITE

☆ ☆ ☆ ☆ ☆

Site Name: ....

Contact Info: ....
....

Fees: ....

Dates: ....

Amenities: ....
....
....

Nearby: ....
....

Traveled With/Met: ....
....
....

Weather:

Conditions: ....

Trip Highlights: ....
....
....

Special Conditions/Needs: ....
....

Likes: ....
....
....

Dislikes: ....
....

Notes for Next Time: ....
....
....

THOUGHTS / NOTES / MEMORIES

CAMPGROUND/SITE

☆ ☆ ☆ ☆ ☆

Site Name: ....

Contact Info: ....

....

Fees: ....

Dates: ....

Amenities: ....

....

....

Nearby: ....

....

Traveled With/Met: ....

....

....

Weather: ☀ ☁ ⛅ 🌧 🌨 🌬 🌡 🌡

Conditions: ....

Trip Highlights: ....
....
....

Special Conditions/Needs: ....
....

Likes: ....
....
....

Dislikes: ....
....

Notes for Next Time: ....
....
....

THOUGHTS / NOTES / MEMORIES

CAMPGROUND/SITE

☆ ☆ ☆ ☆ ☆

Site Name: ....

Contact Info: ....
....

Fees: ....

Dates: ....

Amenities: ....
....
....

Nearby: ....
....

Traveled With/Met: ....
....
....

Weather:

Conditions: ....

Trip Highlights: ....
....
....

Special Conditions/Needs: ....
....

Likes: ....
....
....

Dislikes: ....
....

Notes for Next Time: ....
....
....

THOUGHTS / NOTES / MEMORIES

SKETCHES / MAPS

Part Three

PLACES I'VE BEEN

We all dream of far-off places, and many of us set goals for climbing the tallest peaks, visiting every park in our state, or traveling to special camping spots. Here are some places to check off your list—with room to add your own bucket-list adventures.

US STATES

☐ Alabama	☐ Montana
☐ Alaska	☐ Nebraska
☐ Arizona	☐ Nevada
☐ Arkansas	☐ New Hampshire
☐ California	☐ New Jersey
☐ Colorado	☐ New Mexico
☐ Connecticut	☐ New York
☐ Delaware	☐ North Carolina
☐ Florida	☐ North Dakota
☐ Georgia	☐ Ohio
☐ Hawaii	☐ Oklahoma
☐ Idaho	☐ Oregon
☐ Illinois	☐ Pennsylvania
☐ Indiana	☐ Rhode Island
☐ Iowa	☐ South Carolina
☐ Kansas	☐ South Dakota
☐ Kentucky	☐ Tennessee
☐ Louisiana	☐ Texas
☐ Maine	☐ Utah
☐ Maryland	☐ Vermont
☐ Massachusetts	☐ Virginia
☐ Michigan	☐ Washington
☐ Minnesota	☐ West Virginia
☐ Mississippi	☐ Wisconsin
☐ Missouri	☐ Wyoming

PROVINCES OF CANADA

- ☐ Alberta
- ☐ British Columbia
- ☐ Manitoba
- ☐ New Brunswick
- ☐ Newfoundland and Labrador
- ☐ Northwest Territories
- ☐ Nova Scotia
- ☐ Nunavut
- ☐ Ontario
- ☐ Prince Edward Island
- ☐ Quebec
- ☐ Saskatchewan
- ☐ Yukon

US NATIONAL PARKS

- ☐ Acadia
- ☐ National Park of American Samoa
- ☐ Arches
- ☐ Badlands
- ☐ Big Bend
- ☐ Biscayne
- ☐ Black Canyon of the Gunnison
- ☐ Bryce Canyon
- ☐ Canyonlands
- ☐ Capitol Reef
- ☐ Carlsbad Caverns
- ☐ Channel Islands
- ☐ Congaree
- ☐ Crater Lake
- ☐ Cuyahoga Valley
- ☐ Death Valley
- ☐ Denali
- ☐ Dry Tortugas
- ☐ Everglades
- ☐ Gates of the Arctic
- ☐ Gateway Arch
- ☐ Glacier
- ☐ Glacier Bay
- ☐ Grand Canyon
- ☐ Grand Teton
- ☐ Great Basin
- ☐ Great Sand Dunes
- ☐ Great Smoky Mountains
- ☐ Guadalupe Mountains
- ☐ Haleakalā
- ☐ Hawai'i Volcanoes
- ☐ Hot Springs
- ☐ Indiana Dunes
- ☐ Isle Royale

- [ ] Joshua Tree
- [ ] Katmai
- [ ] Kenai Fjords
- [ ] Kings Canyon
- [ ] Kobuk Valley
- [ ] Lake Clark
- [ ] Lassen Volcanic
- [ ] Mammoth Cave
- [ ] Mesa Verde
- [ ] Mount Rainier
- [ ] New River Gorge
- [ ] North Cascades
- [ ] Olympic
- [ ] Petrified Forest
- [ ] Pinnacles
- [ ] Redwood
- [ ] Rocky Mountain
- [ ] Saguaro
- [ ] Sequoia
- [ ] Shenandoah
- [ ] Theodore Roosevelt
- [ ] Virgin Islands
- [ ] Voyageurs
- [ ] White Sands
- [ ] Wind Cave
- [ ] Wrangell–St. Elias
- [ ] Yellowstone
- [ ] Yosemite
- [ ] Zion

CANADIAN NATIONAL PARKS

- [ ] Akami-Uapishk^{U}-KakKasuak-Mealy Mountains
- [ ] Aulavik
- [ ] Auyuittuq
- [ ] Banff
- [ ] Bruce Peninsula
- [ ] Cape Breton Highlands
- [ ] Elk Island
- [ ] Forillon
- [ ] Fundy
- [ ] Georgian Bay
- [ ] Glacier
- [ ] Grasslands
- [ ] Gros Morne
- [ ] Gulf Islands
- [ ] Gwaii Haanas
- [ ] Ivvavik
- [ ] Jasper
- [ ] Kejimkujik
- [ ] Kluane
- [ ] Kootenay
- [ ] Kouchibouguac

- [ ] La Mauricie
- [ ] Mingan Archipelago
- [ ] Mount Revelstoke
- [ ] Nááts'ihch'oh
- [ ] Nahanni
- [ ] Pacific Rim
- [ ] Point Pelee
- [ ] Prince Albert
- [ ] Prince Edward Island
- [ ] Pukaskwa
- [ ] Qausuittuq
- [ ] Quttinirpaaq
- [ ] Riding Mountain
- [ ] Rouge
- [ ] Sable Island
- [ ] Sirmilik
- [ ] Terra Nova
- [ ] Thaidene Nene
- [ ] Thousand Islands
- [ ] Torngat Mountains
- [ ] Tuktut Nogait
- [ ] Ukkusiksalik
- [ ] Vuntut
- [ ] Wapusk
- [ ] Waterton Lakes
- [ ] Wood Buffalo
- [ ] Yoho

MOUNTAINS

WATERFALLS

HIKING TRAILS

DREAM DESTINATIONS

- [ ] ....
- [ ] ....
- [ ] ....
- [ ] ....
- [ ] ....
- [ ] ....
- [ ] ....
- [ ] ....
- [ ] ....
- [ ] ....
- [ ] ....
- [ ] ....
- [ ] ....
- [ ] ....
- [ ] ....
- [ ] ....
- [ ] ....
- [ ] ....
- [ ] ....
- [ ] ....

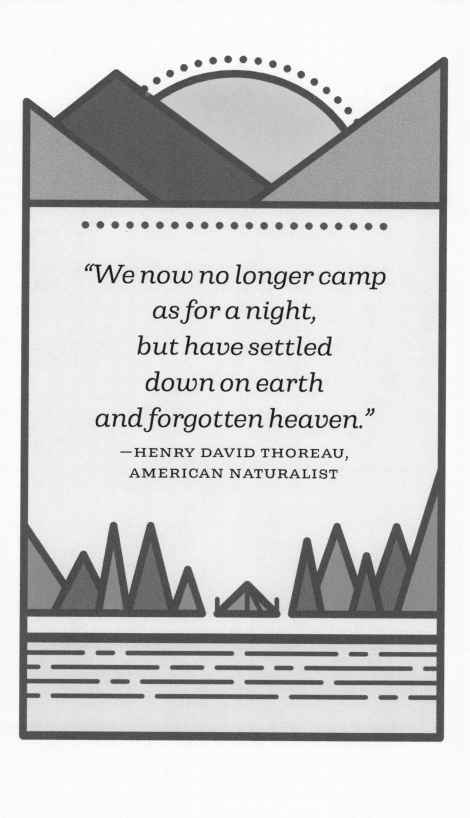

"We now no longer camp
as for a night,
but have settled
down on earth
and forgotten heaven."
—HENRY DAVID THOREAU,
AMERICAN NATURALIST

RESOURCES

MONTyBOCA.com—MONTyBOCA is an online resource for camping and backpacking recipes that are easy to make.

LNT.org—Learn more about the ethics and principles of Leave No Trace. This site also includes helpful tips.

REI.com—REI isn't just a store. They have helpful tricks and tips for all types of camping and also provide many classes for campers.

TalesOfAMountainMama.com—This is a good source of information for family camping.

ACKNOWLEDGMENTS

I just want to say a quick thank-you to everyone who made this journal possible: my husband and my children; the amazing staff at Callisto, including Georgia Freedman and Gurvinder Gandu; and all of my fantastic readers who keep coming back for more.

ABOUT THE AUTHOR

 **Pauline Reynolds-Nuttall** lives on a mountain in the gorgeous Bitterroot Mountains in Montana with her husband, three children, two dogs, chickens, and the occasional black bear or mountain lion. She was raised in both Montana and Israel but is finally back home in the mountains and gullies of her childhood. During the day, Pauline works in human services helping others, and at night she writes about her love for the outdoors. She loves fishing, hiking, backpacking, and camping. This is her second book; she previously wrote the *Cast-Iron Camping Cookbook*. You can find her online at MamaBearOutdoors.com and on Facebook, Twitter, Instagram, and Pinterest @MamaBearOutdoors.